Only the Waves

Also by Judith E.P. Johnson

Mountain Moods (VDL Publications, 1997)
Gatherers (VDL Publications, 1998)
Fragments (VDL Publications, 2000)
Selected Poems CD (7 RPH, 2001)
Snapshot (Regal Press, 2003)
Landmarks (Ginninderra Press, 2005)
Alone at the Window (Ginninderra Press, 2012)
Between Two Moons (Ginninderra Press, 2015)
Waking from Dreams (Ginninderra Press, 2016)
Where It Leads (Ginninderra Press, 2018)

Judith E.P. Johnson

Only the Waves
haiku & senryu

Acknowledgements

The author has had many haiku presented in journals, on radio, and online. The haiku in *Only the Waves* are new and unpublished, except for three that appeared in *Prospect*, *Windfall* and *Ko*.

Special thanks are due to Peter Macrow for his kindness and inspiration; to my children Karen, Debra and Craig, for their encouragement and support; to Jane Williams for editing this book; and to Katherine Johnson for the cover design.

Only the Waves: haiku & senryu
ISBN 978 1 76041 724 6
Copyright © text Judith E.P. Johnson 2019
Cover: Katherine Johnson

First published 2019 by
GINNINDERRA PRESS
PO Box 3461 Port Adelaide SA 5015
www.ginninderrapress.com.au

for Graeme

stars and fireworks
I put up
the new calendar

reading haiku
after dinner
the candle gutters

embers
in the hearth
pine cone glowing

reading *The Pillow Book*
a past life
in your voice

sunrise
through fruit trees
a beehive

dripping leaves
at first light
the smell of earth

playing with grandchild
a hibiscus
behind my ear

spilt cordial
how quickly
the ants have found it

white Easter daisies
garden mist
of childhood

caterpillar
will I know you
in the spring?

gulls circle
the sun
children cartwheeling

long shadows
treetops touch
the tideline

old shed
the passionfruit vine
holds it together

seedling
she tucks its roots
into the flower bed

window web
a spider
against the sky

so many beaches
cowrie shells
in a glass jar

distant roar
through she-oaks
the briny sea

Lady Nelson moored
the mast flashes
the sun on and off

dalmatian
children count and re-count
the spots

car headlights
come and go
child waits at the window

cat on the fence
back and forth
dog fetches a stick

seven candles
on my cake
one for each decade

candles blown out
a whiff
of childhood birthdays

firelight
flickering around the room
my shadow

morning walk
after the clipping
a new dog

heavy frost
old husky
spins all around the lawn

picking up windfall apples
the sun
comes and goes

blossom radiance
old tree
what is your secret?

between Luke and John
in the family Bible
grandpa's baby curl

in velvet and lace
great-grandmother's wax doll
still new

at his funeral
all those relatives
never seen

spring
filling my kitchen
Daphne from your garden

birdsong
at daybreak
coos from the bassinet

this old glove
the shape
of your hand

beachcombing
after the storm
we step over logs

ebb tide
a rock pool
fills with light

cairn
on a shipwreck grave
the wind has taken their names

bush motel pool
a water dragon
swims alone

mountain twilight
valley darkness
deepens

night stillness
outdoor lamp
flickers with moths

cry
from a broken grave
a bird flies out

late sun
a pattern of branches
on fallen leaves

old cubby house
a child looks out
from chicken wire

high dunes
how long have they been here
these midden shells?

whelk at my ear
sound of the sea
in my heartbeat

baby in my arms
her little feet
so far to go

toy zoo
seal's bigger
than the lion

children gone
winged snow angel
left behind

doll's house tea set
the cup
holds a drop

listening
she warms her hands
on the teapot

dripping garden tap
the tub overflows
with mint

twilight
the tawny frogmouth
on which old fence post?

on a moonlit branch
the two owls
we heard

museum silence
only the creak of a chair
in a room of birds

walking to his girlfriend's house
the student
picks a rose

barking dog
the boyfriend steals
a kiss

convalescent walk
we stop
to pick lavender

seniors arm-in-arm
'have a great day girls'
says a young man

warm café
out of the sleety wind
we eat ice cream

studio album
these sepia people
no one knows their story

family stories
your voice
in the retelling

sun-scented
every which way
spring breezes

cloudburst
the big voice
of a little frog

after you've gone
moments you left
in photographs

where
in clear blue skies
last night's stars

call gone
from suburban streets
the postman's whistle

long flight
travelling with me
my thoughts

alone
I listen to mynas
call to each other

buckets of daffodils
outside the florist
July sunshine

beach barbecue
seagulls louder
than the children

after the child
rocking horse
still rocking

fresh from your kitchen
mother's Christmas cake
thirty years on

welcoming guests
tinsel
on the dog's collar

late drive home
children count
the Christmas trees

awake
in the night
daydreaming

in the milky way
one-forty billion stars
my mind is too small

haiku in the sand
only the waves
remember

www.ingramcontent.com/pod-product-compliance
Lightning Source LLC
Chambersburg PA
CBHW062206100526
44589CB00014B/1975